Hot

contents

Key to recipes

SERVES two | 000 | 0 | 0

Calories | Checks | Fat grams

All values given in the recipes are for calories, Checks and grams of fat (in that order), excluding No-Check foods, and are **per serving** unless stated otherwise.

Mediterranean Hot Spots

SERVES two | 345 | 14 | 4

Aromatic rocket & chilli pasta

Prep: **5** mins Cook: **10** mins

175 g/6 oz linguine (dry weight)
spray olive oil
1 red chilli, deseeded and sliced
2 garlic cloves, crushed
finely grated zest and juice of 1 lemon
4 sun-blush tomatoes, drained and chopped
1 small packet wild rocket leaves, roughly chopped
handful of basil leaves
salt and finely ground black pepper
2 tablespoons grated Parmesan cheese

1 Bring a large pan of salted water to a rolling boil and then add the linguine. Boil for about 10 minutes or until the pasta is just tender but still retains some 'bite' (al dente). Drain well.

2 While the pasta is cooking, heat a pan that has been sprayed with oil and, when hot, add the chilli, garlic and lemon zest. Cook for 1 minute without colouring the garlic and then add the lemon juice, sun-blush tomatoes, rocket and basil. Toss lightly for 1-2 minutes to heat through and allow the leaves to wilt.

3 Stir in the drained pasta and Parmesan and season to taste. Serve immediately. This goes well with plain grilled chicken or fish.

Sicilian penne arabbiata

SERVES two | 365 | 15 | 2

Prep: **10** mins Cook: **25** mins

1 small onion, finely chopped
2 garlic cloves, crushed
1 small red pepper, deseeded and chopped
spray oil
2 chillies, chopped
1 x 400 g/14 oz can chopped tomatoes
4 black olives, pitted and chopped
150 ml/¼ pint red wine
pinch of sugar
few drops balsamic vinegar
few sprigs of basil, torn
salt and freshly ground black pepper
175 g/6 oz penne (dry weight)
2 tablespoons chopped parsley

1 Cook the onion, garlic and red pepper in a saucepan that has been sprayed with oil until softened but not coloured.

2 Add the chillies, stir well and cook for 1 minute. Stir in the tomatoes, olives, red wine and sugar, and increase the heat. When the sauce starts to boil, turn it down and simmer gently for about 10-15 minutes until the sauce reduces and thickens.

3 Add the balsamic vinegar and let it bubble away for a few more minutes, then stir in the basil and season to taste.

4 Cook the penne in a large pan of boiling salted water according to the manufacturer's instructions, until just tender. Drain and toss gently in the sauce.

5 Divide the pasta between 2 serving plates and serve sprinkled with parsley. Grilled vegetables or a crisp salad make a good accompaniment.

SERVES two | 340 | 14 | 9

Harissa chicken with falafels

Prep: **15** mins Chill: **30** mins Cook: **20** mins

2 x 150 g/5 oz boneless chicken breasts, skinned
1 level teaspoon harissa paste
juice of ½ lemon
1 tablespoon chopped fresh parsley

Chick pea falafels:

1 x 400 g/14 oz can chick peas, drained
½ small onion, chopped
1 garlic clove, chopped
½ teaspoon ground cumin
½ teaspoon ground coriander
2 tablespoons chopped parsley
¼ teaspoon baking powder
1 egg, beaten
salt and freshly ground black pepper
spray oil

1 Slash the sides of the chicken breasts 2 or 3 times and rub the harissa paste and lemon juice all over them, working the spicy mixture into the cuts. Cover and then chill in the refrigerator for at least ½ hour.

2 Put the chick peas, onion, garlic, spices, parsley and baking powder in a blender or food processor and process to a rough paste. Stir in the beaten egg and seasoning.

3 Divide the mixture into 4 portions and shape each one with your hands into a patty. Chill in the refrigerator for ½ hour until firm.

4 Cook the chicken for about 10 minutes each side under a hot grill, until it is thoroughly cooked.

5 Meanwhile, heat a frying pan that has been sprayed lightly with oil and cook the falafel patties for about 8-10 minutes, turning them frequently, until golden brown and crisp all over.

6 Serve the falafels with the harissa chicken sprinkled with chopped parsley.

Moroccan spiced chicken

SERVES two | 270 | 11 | 4

Prep: **15** mins Chill: **30** mins Cook: **25** mins

- 2 x 150 g/5 oz boneless chicken breasts, skinned
- grated zest and juice of 1 lemon
- few sprigs fresh coriander, finely chopped
- 2 garlic cloves, crushed
- pinch each of ground cumin and cinnamon
- salt and freshly ground black pepper
- spray oil
- lettuce leaves, to serve

Tabbouleh:

- 60 g/2 oz bulghur wheat, soak in cold water for 30 mins
- 2 spring onions, finely chopped
- 2 tomatoes, skinned and chopped
- 3 tablespoons chopped parsley
- 3 tablespoons chopped mint
- juice of ½ lemon
- 1 teaspoon olive oil
- salt and freshly ground black pepper

1 Put the chicken breasts between 2 sheets of greaseproof paper and beat with a rolling pin until flat and thin.

2 In a shallow container, mix together the lemon zest and juice, coriander, garlic, ground spices and seasoning. Place the flattened chicken breasts in this marinade mixture, turning to coat them all over. Cover and leave in the refrigerator for at least 30 minutes.

3 Roll up the marinated chicken breasts like cigars. Secure with wooden cocktail sticks and place them in a baking pan which has been lightly sprayed with oil.

4 Bake in a preheated oven at 200°C/Gas Mark 6 for about 25 minutes, until golden brown and cooked.

5 While the chicken is cooking, make the tabbouleh. Drain the bulghur wheat in a sieve and then squeeze dry. Mix in a bowl with all the other ingredients, checking the seasoning.

6 Serve the cooked spiced chicken with the tabbouleh and some crisp lettuce leaves.

SERVES two | 280 | 11 | 13

Spice crusted lamb with pepper relish

Prep: **15** mins Chill: **1** hr Cook: **20** mins

2 x 150 g/5 oz lamb fillets, all visible fat removed
1 teaspoon coriander seeds
1 teaspoon cumin seeds
1 teaspoon black peppercorns
½ teaspoon ground cinnamon
½ teaspoon ground allspice
pinch of cayenne pepper
1 garlic clove, crushed
juice of ½ lemon
1 teaspoon olive oil

Pepper relish:

2 red peppers
1 red chilli
2 tomatoes, skinned
1 garlic clove, crushed
1 teaspoon caraway seeds
1 tablespoon low-fat yoghurt

1 Place the lamb fillets in a shallow dish. Crush the coriander and cumin seeds and peppercorns with a pestle and mortar and press them into the lamb. Sprinkle with the ground spices, cayenne and garlic and drizzle the lemon juice and olive oil over the top.

2 Cover with a lid or some clingfilm and leave in a cool place to marinate for at least 1 hour. Make the pepper relish. Cook the red peppers under a hot grill, turning often, until blistered and blackened.

3 Peel off the skin and discard the seeds. Cut the pepper flesh into pieces and place in a blender or food processor with the chilli, tomatoes, garlic and caraway seeds. Blend to a purée and stir in the yoghurt. Chill until required.

4 Put the lamb fillets in a baking dish and pour over any marinade. Cook in a preheated oven at 200°C/Gas Mark 6 for about 20 minutes, depending on how well cooked you like your lamb. Serve with the pepper relish and some plain boiled rice (4 Checks per 30g dry weight/75g cooked weight) and salad.

Harira soup

SERVES six | 120 | 5 | 1

Prep: **10** mins Cook: **45** mins

1 onion, finely chopped
1 celery stick, chopped
1 carrot, diced
spray oil
1 level teaspoon ground cumin
½ teaspoon ground cinnamon
½ teaspoon ground ginger
115 g/4 oz split red lentils
350 g/12 oz ripe tomatoes, skinned and chopped
1 tablespoon tomato puree
1.2 litres/2 pints vegetable or chicken stock
1 x 400 g/14 oz can chick peas, drained
salt and freshly ground black pepper
2 tablespoons chopped parsley
small bunch fresh coriander, chopped
harissa paste, to serve

1 Cook the onion, celery and carrot in a pan that has been sprayed lightly with oil over a low heat, until the vegetables are softened.

2 Add the spices and lentils and stir well. Cook for 1 minute and then add the tomatoes, tomato purée and stock.

3 Bring to the boil, then reduce the heat and simmer for about 30 minutes. Add the chick peas and continue cooking for another 10 minutes. The soup should have thickened. Season to taste with salt and pepper.

4 Stir in the chopped parsley and coriander just before ladling the soup into serving bowls. Pass round separately a small dish of fiery harissa paste for people to help themselves, but beware - it is very hot and just a dash will go a long way!

Asian Spice

SERVES two | 250 | 10 | 6

chicken tikka masala

Prep: **15** mins Chill: **30** mins Cook: **15** mins

300 g/10 oz skinless chicken breast fillets
150 ml/¼ pint low-fat natural yoghurt
spray oil
½ onion, finely chopped
1 green chilli deseeded and finely sliced
1 teaspoon turmeric
squeeze of tomato purée
salt and freshly ground black pepper
2 tablespoons chopped fresh coriander
lime wedges, to serve

Masala paste:

½ onion, chopped
2 garlic cloves, crushed
2.5 cm/1 in piece fresh root ginger, peeled and chopped
1-2 green chillies, deseeded and chopped
1 teaspoon each ground coriander and cumin
1 tablespoon garam masala
juice of 1 lime

1 Put all the masala paste ingredients in a blender or food processor and blitz to a smooth paste. Place the chicken fillets in a shallow container. Mix the masala paste with 1 tablespoon of the yoghurt and use to coat the chicken. Cover and leave to marinate for at least 30 minutes.

2 Cook the chicken in its marinade on a preheated griddle pan or barbecue or under an overhead grill for about 10-15 minutes, until cooked through.

3 Meanwhile, in a hot pan sprayed with oil, cook the onion and chilli until softened. Add the turmeric, tomato purée and seasoning and then reduce the heat to as low as it will go and stir in the remaining yoghurt. Heat through very gently.

4 Just before serving, stir the coriander into the yoghurt sauce together with the grilled chicken. Garnish with lime wedges and serve with plain boiled rice (4 Checks per 30g dry weight/75g cooked weight).

lamb balti

SERVES two | 325 | 13 | 14

Prep: **10** mins Chill: **30** mins Cook: **25** mins

225 g/8 oz lean lamb steaks or fillet, visible fat removed
225 g/8 oz low-fat natural yoghurt
1 teaspoon turmeric
2 garlic cloves, crushed
spray oil
1 large onion, chopped
2 tomatoes, skinned and chopped
200 g/7 oz balti cooking sauce
juice of 1 lime
salt and freshly ground black pepper
1 tablespoon chopped fresh coriander
lime wedges, to garnish

1 Cut the lamb into bite-sized chunks and place in a shallow dish. Add the yoghurt, turmeric and garlic and mix well together, coating the lamb all over. Cover and leave to marinate in a cool place for at least 30 minutes.

2 Heat a pan that has been sprayed lightly with oil and cook the onion over a low heat until softened.

3 Add the tomatoes and then stir in the balti sauce. Warm through and then add the lamb in its marinade. Continue cooking over a low heat for about 15 minutes until the lamb is thoroughly cooked. Stir in the lime juice and check the seasoning.

4 Scatter the coriander over the top and serve with lime wedges and plain boiled rice (4 Checks per 30g dry weight/75g cooked weight).

SERVES two | 215 | 9 | 6

stir-fried ginger chicken

Prep: **5** mins Cook: **20** mins

spray oil
250 g/9 oz boneless chicken breasts, skinned and cut into chunks
2 garlic cloves, crushed
2.5 cm/1 in piece fresh root ginger, peeled and grated
1 red chilli, deseeded and chopped
2 teaspoons ground coriander
1 teaspoon ground cumin
¼ teaspoon ground turmeric
125 ml/4½ fl oz chicken stock
175 ml/6 fl oz low-fat natural yoghurt
salt and freshly ground black pepper
1 tablespoon chopped fresh coriander
lime pickle and coriander chutney, to serve (optional)

1 Spray a wok or large non-stick frying pan with oil and heat until it is really hot. Add the chicken and stir-fry briskly for 4-5 minutes, until golden all over.

2 Reduce the heat a little and add the garlic, ginger and chilli and cook for 1 minute. Stir in the ground spices and then pour in the chicken stock.

3 Bring to the boil and then reduce the heat and cook for about 10 minutes, until the liquid has reduced and the chicken is cooked.

4 Stir in the yoghurt and warm through gently. Check the seasoning and scatter with coriander before serving with plain boiled rice (4 Checks per 30g dry weight/75g cooked weight) and vegetables. If wished, serve with some Indian pickles.

tikka hoki kebabs

SERVES two | 405 | 16 | 6

Prep: **10** mins Chill: **30** mins Cook: **15** mins

5 tablespoons low-fat natural yoghurt
2 tablespoons tikka curry paste (e.g. Patak's)
juice of ½ lemon
300 g/10 oz hoki fillets, skinned and boned

Saffron rice:

spray oil
1 dried red chilli
4 cardamom pods, crushed
1 cinnamon stick
115 g/4 oz basmati rice
225 ml/8 fl oz boiling water
1 sachet powdered saffron
salt and freshly ground black pepper
1 tablespoon chopped fresh coriander

1 Mix together the yoghurt, tikka curry paste and lemon juice. Cut the hoki into large chunks and stir into the spicy yoghurt mixture. Cover and leave to marinate in a cool place for at least 30 minutes.

2 Make the saffron rice. Heat a pan that has been sprayed with oil and stir-fry the chilli, cardamom pods and cinnamon stick for 2 minutes.

3 Add the rice and stir well for 1-2 minutes. Pour in the boiling water, add the saffron and seasoning and bring to the boil. Reduce the heat to a bare simmer, cover the pan and cook gently for 10 minutes until the rice has absorbed all the liquid and is tender and fluffy.

4 Meanwhile, thread the marinated hoki onto some kebab skewers and cook under a preheated hot grill for 5-6 minutes until the fish is cooked.

5 Serve the fish kebabs on a bed of saffron rice, which has been sprinkled with fresh coriander.

SERVES two | 90 | 4 (8)

kerala vegetable curry

Prep: **10** mins Cook: **30** mins

spray oil
1 teaspoon black mustard seeds
½ teaspoon cumin seeds
¼ teaspoon turmeric
½ teaspoon garam masala
½ teaspoon ground coriander
1 chilli, deseeded and chopped
1 onion, finely chopped
1 garlic clove, crushed
2.5 cm/1 in piece fresh root ginger, grated
115 g/4 oz tomatoes, skinned and chopped
2 courgettes, sliced
1 small aubergine, diced
150 ml/¼ pint reduced-fat coconut milk
60 g/2 oz thin green beans, trimmed and cut in half
salt and freshly ground black pepper

1 Spray a heavy-based pan with oil and place over a medium to high heat. When hot, add the mustard seeds and cook, stirring occasionally, for about 2 minutes until they start popping.

2 Stir in the spices, chilli, onion, garlic and ginger and cook gently over a low heat until the onion is tender and translucent.

3 Add the tomatoes, courgettes and aubergine. Stir well and then pour in the coconut milk. Cook for about 10 minutes and then add the green beans. Continue cooking for another 5 minutes or so until all the vegetables are cooked and tender and the liquid has reduced.

4 Check the seasoning and serve immediately with some plain boiled rice (4 Checks per 30g dry weight/ 75g cooked weight).

spicy indian lentil soup

SERVES six | 150 | 6 | 1

Prep: **10** mins Cook: **35-40** mins

- **1 onion, finely chopped**
- **2.5 cm/1 in piece fresh root ginger, peeled and chopped**
- **2 garlic cloves, crushed**
- **spray oil**
- **2 teaspoons black mustard seeds**
- **½ teaspoon cumin seeds**
- **1 red chilli, finely chopped**
- **1 teaspoon turmeric**
- **225 g/8 oz tomatoes, skinned and chopped**
- **225 g/8 oz split red lentils**
- **1.2 litres/2 pints vegetable stock**
- **salt and freshly ground black pepper**
- **6 teaspoons low-fat natural yoghurt**
- **sprigs of coriander leaves, chopped, to garnish**

1 Gently cook the onion, ginger and garlic until softened but not coloured in a heavy saucepan which has been sprayed with oil.

2 Add the mustard seeds and cook for 2 minutes, until they start to pop. Stir in the cumin, chilli, turmeric, tomatoes and lentils, combining well. Cook for 1 minute.

3 Add the stock and bring to the boil. Reduce the heat and simmer gently for 25-30 minutes, until the lentils are cooked and the soup has thickened. Check the seasoning, adding salt and pepper to taste.

4 You can serve the soup as it is if you like the rough, chunky texture. Alternatively, purée it in a blender or food processor until smooth. Ladle into serving bowls and swirl in a spoonful of yoghurt. Strew with coriander and serve.

Tantalising Thai

lemon grass beef skewers

SERVES two | 210 | 8 | 8

Prep: **15** mins Cook: **10** mins

250 g/9 oz ground lean beef (less than 5 per cent fat)
2 teaspoons garlic paste
1 teaspoon nam pla (Thai fish sauce)
1 teaspoon finely chopped fresh coriander
½ teaspoon brown sugar
8 lemon grass stalks
spray oil
2 dessertspoons sweet chilli sauce, to serve (optional)

Hot radish salad:

small bunch radishes, sliced
¼ cucumber, peeled and cut into matchstick strips
¼ red onion, finely sliced
1 red chilli, deseeded and finely shredded
few fresh coriander leaves, chopped
grated zest and juice of 1 lime
1 tablespoon nam pla (Thai fish sauce)
½ teaspoon brown sugar

1 In a bowl, mix together the ground beef with the garlic paste, nam pla, chopped coriander and brown sugar to make a paste. Divide into 4 equal-sized portions.

2 Take one portion of the beef paste and mould it around a lemon grass stalk. Do the same with the remaining paste and stalks.

3 Spray a non-stick frying pan or griddle with oil and place over a medium heat. When hot, lay the lemon grass skewers in the pan and cook for about 10 minutes, carefully turning them every few minutes, until the beef is thoroughly cooked and browned.

4 While they are cooking make the salad. Put the radishes, cucumber, red onion, chilli and coriander in a bowl. Mix together the remaining ingredients and toss gently with the salad.

5 Arrange the salad on 2 serving plates and place the lemon grass skewers on top. Serve with plain boiled rice (4 Checks per 30g dry weight/75g cooked weight) and chilli sauce.

SERVES two | 310 | 12 | 9

turkey satay

Prep: **10** mins Chill: **1** hr Cook: **12-15** mins

300 g/10 oz lean turkey meat
1 teaspoon brown sugar
1 teaspoon ground turmeric
1 teaspoon ground coriander
1 teaspoon ground cumin
1 teaspoon Thai red curry paste
4 tablespoons reduced-fat coconut milk
salt and freshly ground black pepper
2 tablespoons chopped fresh coriander
¼ cucumber, cut into chunks
lime wedges

Satay dip:

2 tablespoons satay sauce (e.g. Tesco Finest Stir Fry & Dipping Sauce)
squeeze of lime juice
6 tablespoons virtually fat-free fromage frais

1 Cut the turkey into bite-sized chunks. In a basin, mix together the brown sugar, turmeric, coriander, cumin, curry paste and coconut milk. Season with salt and pepper and add the turkey, turning it in the marinade until completely coated.

2 Cover and leave in the refrigerator or a cool place to marinate for at least 1 hour.

3 Thread the marinated turkey onto thin bamboo skewers. Cook on a barbecue or griddle pan or under a hot grill for about 12-15 minutes, turning them frequently and brushing with the leftover marinade, until golden and slightly charred and the turkey is cooked through inside.

4 While the kebabs are cooking, mix together the satay sauce, lime juice and fromage frais for the dip and spoon into a small bowl.

5 Serve the kebabs, strewn with fresh coriander, with the cucumber chunks and lime wedges. Dip the turkey into the satay dip. Some steamed oriental vegetables, e.g. sugar snap peas and pak choi, go well with this dish.

barbecued chicken drumsticks

SERVES two | 265 | 11 | 9

Prep: **10** mins Chill: **1** hr Cook: **25-30** mins

6 free-range chicken drumsticks, skinned
1 stalk lemon grass, peeled, chopped and crushed
1 garlic clove, crushed
1 red chilli, deseeded and chopped
2.5 cm/1in piece fresh root ginger, peeled, finely chopped
3 tablespoons chopped fresh coriander
grated zest and juice of 1 lime
1 teaspoon sesame or olive oil
sea salt and freshly ground black pepper
salad leaves, to serve

Thai red curry dip:

2 teaspoons Thai red curry paste
5 tablespoons virtually fat-free fromage frais

1 Slash the meat of the chicken drumsticks 2 or 3 times with a sharp knife. Arrange them in a shallow dish.

2 Mix together the lemon grass, garlic, chilli, ginger, coriander, lime zest and juice and oil. Season with salt and pepper and spoon over the chicken drumsticks, rubbing the marinade well into the slashes.

3 Cover the dish with a lid or clingfilm and leave to marinate in the refrigerator or a cool place for at least 1 hour to allow the flavours to develop.

4 Cook the coated chicken under a preheated hot grill or, even better, over glowing hot coals on a barbecue for about 25-30 minutes until it is thoroughly cooked and the juices run clear when it is pierced with a skewer. Turn the chicken frequently to cook it evenly and colour it all over. If it looks dry, baste with the leftover marinade.

5 Blend the red curry paste with the fromage frais and place in a small dish.

6 Serve the chicken on a bed of salad leaves with the Thai red curry dip. Some plain boiled Thai fragrant rice (4 Checks per 30g dry weight/75g cooked weight) or grilled naan bread (8 Checks 7g fat per 60g/2oz mini naan) go well with this dish.

SERVES two | 200 | 8 | 14

fusion spicy scrambled eggs

Prep: **3** mins Cook: **7-8** mins

spray oil
1 red chilli, deseeded and finely chopped
2 spring onions, thinly sliced
4 large free-range organic eggs
salt and freshly ground black pepper
1 ripe tomato, skinned, deseeded and chopped
3 tablespoons chopped fresh coriander

1 Lightly spray a non-stick saucepan with oil and place over a medium heat. When hot, add the chilli and spring onions and cook for 2-3 minutes, until softened.

2 With a fork or a balloon whisk, beat the eggs with a tablespoon of cold water and the seasoning until well combined, and pour into the pan on top of the onions and chilli.

3 Cook over a low heat, stirring well with a wooden spoon to prevent the eggs sticking to the base of the pan.

4 While the scrambled eggs are still moist, just before they set, add the tomato and chopped coriander. Continue stirring until the mixture is creamy and set.

5 Serve immediately on warm serving plates with some grilled mushrooms and tomatoes.

stir-fried prawns & noodles

SERVES two | 340 | 14 | 1

Prep: **10** mins Cook: **15** mins

- **125 g/4½ oz rice noodles**
- **spray oil**
- **4 spring onions, shredded**
- **1 garlic clove, crushed**
- **1 teaspoon shredded fresh root ginger**
- **85 g/3 oz sugar-snap peas, trimmed**
- **200 g/7 oz raw peeled tiger prawns (fresh or frozen and thawed)**
- **juice of 1 lime**
- **1 tablespoon nam pla (Thai fish sauce)**
- **1 tablespoon sweet chilli sauce**
- **2 tablespoons chopped fresh coriander**

1 Cook the rice noodles, according to the manufacturer's instructions, until tender and then drain well and set aside.

2 Spray a large non-stick frying pan or wok with oil and, when it is really hot, briskly stir-fry the spring onions, garlic and ginger for 2 minutes.

3 Add the sugar-snap peas and stir-fry for 1 minute before stirring in the tiger prawns. Continue stir-frying for about 3 more minutes until they turn pink all over.

4 Add the cooked noodles to the pan with the lime juice, nam pla and sweet chilli sauce. Toss them gently together with the other ingredients in the pan and heat through quickly.

5 Serve immediately scattered with chopped coriander. Pak choi or some spring greens or cabbage make a good accompaniment.

SERVES two | 110 | 4 | 6

thai seafood & coconut soup

Prep: **10** mins Cook: **30** mins

1.2 litres/2 pints fish or vegetable stock
2 stalks lemon grass, peeled, chopped and crushed
2 kaffir lime leaves, rolled up and shredded
2 garlic cloves, crushed
2 small red chillies, deseeded and finely chopped
1 tablespoon nam pla (Thai fish sauce)
4 spring onions, sliced
juice of 1 lime
300 ml/½ pint reduced-fat coconut milk
350 g/12 oz peeled raw tiger prawns (fresh or frozen and thawed)
salt and freshly ground black pepper
small bunch of coriander, chopped

1 Put the stock, lemon grass, lime leaves, garlic, chillies and nam pla in a large saucepan and bring to the boil.

2 Reduce the heat and simmer gently for 10 minutes to allow the flavours to develop and mingle.

3 Add the spring onions, lime juice and coconut milk and cook over a low heat for 10 minutes.

4 Add the tiger prawns and cook gently for another 4-5 minutes until they turn pink. Season to taste with salt and pepper but check before adding the salt as the nam pla makes the soup quite salty.

5 Stir in the chopped coriander and ladle into bowls. Serve piping hot.

Dragon Fire

SERVES two | 405 | 16 | 8

singapore noodles

Prep: **15** mins Cook: **15** mins

- **150 g/5 oz dried egg noodles**
- **1 tablespoon soy sauce**
- **spray oil**
- **3 spring onions, sliced**
- **2 garlic cloves, cut into slivers**
- **1 red chilli, deseeded and shredded**
- **2.5 cm/1 in piece fresh root ginger, peeled & shredded**
- **60 g/2 oz canned bamboo shoots, drained**
- **60 g/2 oz bean sprouts**
- **60 g/2 oz mangetouts, trimmed**
- **200 g/7 oz skinless chicken breast fillets, cut into strips**
- **few sprigs of coriander, torn**
- **1 teaspoon toasted sesame seeds**

Cornflour mixture:

- **2 tablespoons soy sauce**
- **1 tablespoon sweet chilli sauce**
- **125 ml/4½ fl oz water**
- **1 tablespoon cornflour**

1 Cook the egg noodles according to the manufacturer's instructions on the packet and drain well. Toss them in the soy sauce and set aside.

2 Spray a deep frying pan or wok and place over a high heat. Add the spring onions, garlic, chilli, ginger, bamboo shoots, bean sprouts and mangetouts. Stir-fry for 2-3 minutes and then remove from the wok and keep warm.

3 Add the chicken to the wok and stir-fry briskly for 2-3 minutes over a high heat until cooked through and golden brown.

4 Blend the soy sauce, chilli sauce and water together, and then stir in the cornflour. It should be smooth with no lumps.

5 Add the cornflour mixture to the chicken and stir in well. Return the cooked vegetables to the wok with the noodles and stir gently over a low heat until the sauce thickens and everything is hot.

6 Serve sprinkled with coriander and sesame seeds.

szechuan pork chow mein

SERVES two | 500 | 20 | 9

Prep: **15** mins Cook: **15** mins

- **175 g/6 oz dried egg noodles**
- **200 g/7 oz pork fillet, fat removed and cut into thin strips**
- **1 tablespoon soy sauce**
- **spray oil**
- **1 onion, thinly sliced**
- **2 garlic cloves, crushed**
- **1 green chilli, finely chopped**
- **115 g/4 oz bean sprouts**
- **115 g/4 oz mangetouts**
- **1 sachet chow mein sauce (e.g. Blue Dragon)**
- **shredded spring onions, to garnish**

1 Cook the egg noodles according to the manufacturer's instructions on the packet and drain well. Set aside.

2 Toss the strips of pork fillet in the soy sauce until well coated. Spray a deep frying pan or wok and place over a high heat. Add the pork strips and stir-fry for 3-4 minutes until cooked and golden brown. Remove and keep warm.

3 Add the onion, garlic, chilli, bean sprouts and mangetouts to the hot wok and stir-fry for 2-3 minutes.

4 Tip in the drained egg noodles and pork strips and then stir in the chow mein sauce. Heat through for about 2 minutes and then serve scattered with shredded spring onions.

SERVES two 190 8 6

hot & sour crunchy beef salad

Prep: **15** mins Cook: **5** mins

- spray oil
- 250 g/9 oz lean sirloin steak, all visible fat removed
- 8 spring onions, trimmed and halved
- ½ cucumber, cut into matchstick strips
- 1 red chilli, deseeded and shredded
- 60 g/2 oz beansprouts
- 1 small packet baby spinach leaves
- few sprigs of fresh coriander, mint and basil, roughly chopped
- salt and freshly ground black pepper

Oriental dressing:

- 2 tablespoons nam pla (Thai fish sauce)
- 2 tablespoons lime juice
- 2 teaspoons sugar

1 Whisk all the dressing ingredients together until well blended.

2 Cut the steak into thin strips. Lightly spray a ridged griddle pan with oil and heat. When the pan is hot, add the strips of steak and the spring onions. Cook over a high heat to sear them, turning them often. The steak should be browned outside and pink and juicy inside. Season with salt and pepper.

3 Toss the cucumber, chilli, beansprouts, spinach and herbs in the prepared dressing.

4 Add the hot onions and steak strips and toss again to coat them lightly. Serve immediately while the salad is hot.

szechuan chilli beef

SERVES two | 200 | 8 | 6

Prep: **15** mins Cook: **5** mins

- **250 g/9 oz lean sirloin steak, fat removed and thinly sliced**
- **salt and freshly ground black pepper**
- **spray oil**
- **2 red chillies, deseeded and shredded**
- **2 garlic cloves, crushed**
- **2.5 cm/1 in piece fresh root ginger, peeled and chopped**
- **3 spring onions, trimmed and shredded**
- **1 carrot, cut into matchstick strips**
- **1 celery stick, cut into matchstick strips**
- **1 tablespoon soy sauce**
- **1 tablespoon dry sherry or rice wine**
- **1 tablespoon hoisin sauce**

1 Sprinkle the strips of steak with a little salt and plenty of black pepper. Spray a wok or deep frying pan with oil and place over a medium heat.

2 When it is hot, tip in the steak strips and stir-fry briskly for 1 minute to sear them on the outside. Add the chillies, garlic, ginger, spring onions, carrot and celery and stir-fry for 1-2 minutes.

3 Stir in the soy sauce, dry sherry or rice wine and hoisin sauce and cook for 2 minutes.

4 Serve immediately with some plain boiled rice or egg noodles (4 Checks per 30g dry weight/75g cooked weight for either rice or noodles).

SERVES two | 250 | 10 | 2

chinese chicken pancakes

Prep: **10** mins Cook: **8** mins

200 g/7 oz skinless chicken breast fillets, cut into strips
1 tablespoon light soy sauce
spray oil
½ yellow pepper, deseeded and thinly sliced
115 g/4 oz mushrooms, thinly sliced
2 spring onions, chopped
60 g/2 oz bean sprouts
1 sachet Canton black bean stir-fry sauce (e.g. Blue Dragon)
4 Chinese Style Pancakes (available in packs from large supermarkets and Chinese/Oriental grocers)
shredded spring onions, to garnish
2 dessertspoons sweet chilli sauce for dipping

1 Put the chicken strips in a bowl and spoon over the soy sauce. Turn the strips over in the sauce to coat them.

2 Spray a deep frying pan or wok and place over a high heat. Add the soy chicken strips and cook briskly for 2-3 minutes, tossing them in the wok.

3 Add the yellow pepper, mushrooms, spring onions and bean sprouts and stir-fry for 2 minutes. Add the sauce and cook for a further 2 minutes.

4 Meanwhile, cook the pancakes as directed in the manufacturer's instructions on the packet.

5 Place a large spoonful of chicken filling on each pancake and roll up. Serve scattered with shredded spring onions with some sweet chilli sauce on the side.

oriental duck stir-fry

SERVES two | 200 | 8 | 8

Prep: **15** mins Chill: **30** mins Cook: **12** mins

- **2 x 125 g/4½ oz skinless duck breast fillets, fat removed**
- **1 tablespoon soy sauce**
- **2.5 cm/1 in piece fresh root ginger, peeled and grated**
- **spray oil**
- **4 spring onions, sliced diagonally**
- **1 carrot, cut into matchstick strips**
- **½ red pepper, deseeded and cut into thin strips**
- **½ green pepper, deseeded and cut into thin strips**
- **60 g/2 oz mangetouts, trimmed**
- **1 tablespoon sweet chilli sauce**

1 Cut the duck fillets into thin strips and mix in a bowl with the soy sauce and ginger. Cover and leave in the refrigerator to marinate for 30 minutes.

2 Spray a deep frying pan or wok and place over a high heat. Add the duck strips in their marinade to the hot wok and stir-fry for about 4 minutes until cooked through. Remove and keep warm while you cook the vegetables.

3 Add the spring onions, carrot and peppers to the wok and stir-fry for 3-4 minutes. Add the mangetouts and cook for 1 minute.

4 Return the duck to the pan and stir in the chilli sauce. Heat through and serve immediately with cooked Chinese egg noodles (4 Checks per 30 g dry weight/ 75 g cooked weight).

Tex-Mex Temptation

SERVES two | 300 | 12 | 10

sizzling vegetable fajitas

Prep: **15** mins Cook: **15** mins

spray oil
1 red onion, sliced
½ red pepper, deseeded and sliced
½ yellow pepper, deseeded and sliced
½ green pepper, deseeded and sliced
1 red chilli, finely sliced
115 g/4 oz chestnut mushrooms, thinly sliced
salt and freshly ground black pepper
4 small warmed tortillas
2 tablespoons chopped fresh coriander
4 teaspoons tomato salsa
4 teaspoons low-fat guacamole

1 Spray a ridged griddle pan or frying pan with oil and place over a medium heat. When hot, add the onion, peppers and chilli and cook, turning occasionally, for about 8-10 minutes until softened.

2 Add the chestnut mushrooms and cook for 2-3 minutes. Season to taste with salt and pepper and turn up the heat briefly until everything is sizzling.

3 Divide the mixture between 4 warmed tortillas and top each one with some chopped coriander and a spoonful of salsa and one of guacamole.

4 Fold over or roll up and serve immediately with a tomato salad.

buffalo wings

SERVES two | 150 | 6 | 2

Prep: **15** mins Chill: **30** mins Cook: **20-25** mins

2 tablespoons soy sauce
1 tablespoon tomato ketchup
1 teaspoon wine or cider vinegar
2 teaspoons liquid honey
1 red chilli, deseeded and finely chopped
2 garlic cloves, crushed
1 teaspoon paprika
8 chicken wings on the bone, skinned
snipped chives, to garnish
lemon wedges and salad leaves, to serve

Honey mustard sauce:

100 ml/3½ fl oz virtually fat-free fromage frais
2 level teaspoons whole-grain mustard
grated zest of 1 lemon
1 teaspoon liquid honey

1 In a bowl, mix together the soy sauce, tomato ketchup, vinegar, honey, chilli, garlic and paprika. Place the chicken wings in this mixture and turn them until they are well coated.

2 Cover and leave in the refrigerator to marinate for at least 30 minutes.

3 Remove the chicken wings and place them in a large baking dish. Pour any leftover marinade over them and cook in a preheated oven at 200°C/Gas Mark 6 for 20-25 minutes until the chicken is thoroughly cooked, appetizingly golden brown and sticky.

4 While the chicken is cooking, mix together the ingredients for the honey mustard sauce.

5 Serve the buffalo wings sprinkled with snipped chives with lemon wedges on a bed of crisp salad leaves. Eat with your fingers, dipping them into the honey mustard sauce.

SERVES two | 70 | 3 | 1

acapulco prawns with tomato sauce

Prep: **10** mins Cook: **25** mins

- spray oil
- 1 onion, finely chopped
- 3 garlic cloves, crushed
- 1 green chilli, finely chopped
- 3 tablespoons chopped fresh parsley
- 3 large tomatoes, skinned and chopped
- 1 tablespoon tomato purée
- juice of 1 lime
- 100 ml/3½ fl oz vegetable or fish stock
- 250 g/9 oz unpeeled raw tiger prawns
- salt and freshly ground black pepper
- sprigs of flat-leaf parsley, to garnish
- lime wedges

1 Spray a large non-stick frying pan with oil and cook the onion and garlic until softened and golden. Add the chilli and chopped parsley and cook for about 2 minutes, until the parsley turns dark green.

2 Add the tomatoes, tomato purée and lime juice, and simmer for about 10 minutes until thick and reduced. Season to taste with salt and pepper.

3 Pour in the stock and simmer for 5 minutes, then add the prawns. Cook for 2-3 minutes, turning them occasionally, until they become pink.

4 Serve the prawns in their sauce with some plain boiled rice (4 Checks per 30g dry weight/75g cooked weight). Garnish with sprigs of parsley and lime wedges.

chicken kebabs with avocado and pomegranates

SERVES two | 295 | 12 | 14

Prep: **20** mins Chill: **30** mins Cook: **15** mins

- juice of 2 limes or 1 lemon
- 1 green chilli, finely chopped
- 1 teaspoon honey
- 200 g/7 oz skinless chicken breast fillets
- salt and freshly ground black pepper
- seeds of 1 pomegranate
- sprigs of fresh basil

Avocado sauce:

- 1 teaspoon olive oil
- 1 teaspoon wine or cider vinegar
- 1 teaspoon sweet chilli sauce
- 1 small ripe avocado, peeled and stoned
- 1 ripe tomato, skinned and chopped
- 2 spring onions, chopped
- 5 tablespoons virtually fat-free fromage frais

1 Squeeze the lime or lemon juice into a bowl and stir in the chilli and honey. Cut the chicken into bite-sized chunks and stir into this marinade. Cover and chill in the refrigerator for at least 30 minutes.

2 Thread the chicken onto some bamboo skewers. Brush with the marinade and cook under a preheated hot grill or on a barbecue, turning occasionally, for about 15 minutes until thoroughly cooked and golden brown.

3 While the chicken is cooking, make the avocado sauce. Blend the oil and vinegar together in a bowl with the chilli sauce. Mash the avocado flesh and beat into the spicy oil and vinegar mixture. Stir in the tomato, spring onions and fromage frais.

4 Season the cooked kebabs with salt and pepper and arrange on serving plates. Serve with a mound of avocado sauce, sprinkled with fresh pomegranate seeds and garnished with basil.

SERVES two | 270 | 11 | 11

garbanzos

Prep: **15** mins Cook: **20** mins

60 g/2 oz lean bacon lardons
1 onion, finely chopped
2 garlic cloves, crushed
1 red pepper, deseeded and chopped
1 dried hot red chilli, crumbled
300 g/10 oz ripe tomatoes, skinned and chopped
½ teaspoon dried oregano
1 x 400 g/14 oz can chick peas, drained
salt and freshly ground black pepper
2 tablespoons chopped fresh coriander

1 Put the bacon lardons in a hot frying pan and dry-fry until golden and the fat runs out of them. Drain off the fat.

2 Add the onion, garlic and red pepper to the bacon in the pan and cook over a low heat for about 5 minutes until softened.

3 Crumble in the chilli and stir in the tomatoes and oregano with the chick peas. Season to taste with salt and pepper and simmer for 10 minutes, stirring occasionally, until thickened.

4 Stir in the chopped coriander and serve with some boiled rice (4 Checks per 30g dry weight/75g cooked weight) or tortillas (6 Checks 4g fat per average 60g/2oz flour tortilla) and grilled vegetables.

spicy tex-mex chicken pockets

SERVES two | 270 | 11 | 4

Prep: **15** mins Cook: **10** mins

200 g/7 oz skinless chicken breast fillets
spray oil
2 garlic cloves, sliced
1 red chilli, deseeded and shredded
1 red onion, sliced
1 red pepper, deseeded and sliced
1 courgette, sliced
salt and freshly ground black pepper
2 pitta breads
2 teaspoons tomato salsa
2 teaspoons virtually fat-free fromage frais
few sprigs of coriander, chopped

1 Cut the chicken into bite-sized chunks and cook for 2-3 minutes over a high heat in a ridged griddle pan which has been sprayed lightly with oil - just long enough to sear the chicken all over.

2 Add the garlic, chilli, red onion, pepper and courgette and cook for about 5 minutes, stirring occasionally, until the chicken is cooked and golden brown and the vegetables are softened and slightly charred. Season to taste with salt and pepper.

3 Meanwhile, warm the pitta breads in a low oven. Split each one down the side to form a pocket and fill with the chicken and vegetable mixture.

4 Add some salsa and fromage frais to each pitta pocket and sprinkle with coriander. Serve hot with a crisp salad.

Caribbean Kick

jamaican jerked chicken

SERVES two | 210 | 8 | 3

Prep: **15** mins Chill: **1** hr Cook: **25-30** mins

2 x 150 g/5 oz skinless, boned chicken breasts
cherry tomatoes, to serve

Jerk mixture:

2 spring onions, finely sliced
1 garlic clove, crushed
½ teaspoon red chilli paste
½ teaspoon ground allspice
¼ teaspoon cinnamon
good pinch of grated fresh nutmeg
grated zest and juice of 1 lime
freshly ground black pepper

Papaya salsa:

1 ripe papaya, peeled, deseeded and diced
2 spring onions, finely chopped
1 small red chilli, deseeded and chopped
juice of 1 lime
few sprigs of mint, chopped

1 Mix all the ingredients together for the jerk mixture. Slash each chicken breast 2 or 3 times with a sharp knife and rub the jerk mixture over it, especially into the slashes.

2 Cover the chicken breasts and chill in the refrigerator for at least 1 hour.

3 Place the chicken breasts in a baking pan and spoon over any leftover jerk mixture. Bake in a preheated oven at 200°C/Gas Mark 6 for 25-30 minutes. The chicken is cooked when the juices run clear when pierced with a knife. If preferred, you can grill it instead.

4 While the chicken is cooking, mix the papaya salsa ingredients together.

5 Serve the jerked chicken with the papaya salsa and some cherry tomatoes and plain boiled rice (4 Checks per 30 g dry weight/75 g cooked weight).

SERVES two | 310 | 12 | 12

chicken with cinnamon glazed plantains

Prep: **15** mins Cook: **25** mins

2 x 150 g/5 oz skinless, boned chicken breasts
spray oil
1 red onion, cut into wedges

Cinnamon glazed plantains:

1 ripe plantain, peeled
1 teaspoon ground cinnamon
1 teaspoon liquid honey

Avocado salsa:

1 small ripe avocado, peeled, stoned and diced
2 ripe tomatoes, chopped
½ small red onion, diced
1 red chilli, deseeded and chopped
juice of ½ lemon
2 tablespoons chopped fresh coriander

1 Make the avocado salsa. Combine all the ingredients in a small bowl, then cover and chill in the refrigerator until required.

2 Place the chicken breasts on a hot griddle pan which has been sprayed lightly with oil. Cook over a medium to high heat for about 25 minutes, turning them occasionally, until golden brown and thoroughly cooked.

3 After 15 minutes, add the red onion wedges to the pan. Grill, turning them often, until they are softened, slightly caramelized and charred.

4 While the chicken is cooking, put the plantain in a baking dish and sprinkle with cinnamon, then drizzle with honey. Bake in a preheated oven at 180°C/Gas Mark 4 for 10-12 minutes.

5 Serve the chicken and red onion wedges with some avocado salsa. Cut the plantain in half lengthwise and place one half on each plate.

callaloo

SERVES six | 150 | 6 | 6

Prep: **15** mins Cook: **40** mins

1 onion, finely chopped
2 garlic cloves, crushed
spray oil
1 fresh red chilli, deseeded and sliced
1 teaspoon ground turmeric
1 medium potato, peeled and diced
350 g/12 oz spinach leaves, trimmed and chopped
4 ripe tomatoes, skinned and chopped
900 ml/1½ pints vegetable stock
300 ml/½ pint reduced-fat coconut milk
1 x 400 g/14 oz pack frozen fruits de mer (mixed seafood), thawed
salt and freshly ground black pepper
juice of 1 lime
dash of hot pepper sauce
3 tablespoons chopped fresh parsley

1 Cook the onion and garlic until softened in a large saucepan which has been sprayed lightly with oil.

2 Add the chilli, turmeric and potato and cook for 2 minutes, then tip in the spinach leaves and cook, stirring, for 2 more minutes until they turn bright green and wilt.

3 Add the tomatoes and vegetable stock and simmer for about 20 minutes.

4 Add the coconut milk together with the thawed fruits de mer and their liquid. Heat through gently and cook for about 10 minutes. Season with salt and pepper and stir in the lime juice and hot pepper sauce to taste.

5 Ladle the hot soup into serving bowls and sprinkle with some chopped parsley.

SERVES two | 255 | 10 | 8

snapper fillets with mango chilli sauce

Prep: **20** mins Cook: **40** mins

2 x 175 g/6 oz red snapper or sea bass fillets
salt and freshly ground black pepper
spray oil
1 red chilli, deseeded and shredded
few chives, to garnish
lime wedges

Mango chilli sauce:

1 red pepper, deseeded and chopped
4 skinned tomatoes, deseeded and chopped
1 ripe mango, peeled, stoned and cubed
1 hot Scotch bonnet chilli, deseeded and chopped
3 tablespoons cider vinegar
1 tablespoon brown sugar
½ teaspoon Dijon mustard
pinch of ground cinnamon
pinch of ground cumin
salt and freshly ground black pepper

1 Make the mango chilli sauce. Put all the ingredients in a saucepan and simmer gently for about 30 minutes until everything is cooked and softened. Check the sauce occasionally to make sure it is not getting too dry. If so, add a little cold water to moisten it.

2 Tip the sauce into a blender or food processor and blitz to a smooth purée.

3 Season the red snapper fillets with salt and pepper. Spray a frying pan or griddle pan lightly with oil and when it is really hot, add the fish fillets. Cook over a medium heat, skin side down, until crisp and golden, then flip them over and cook the other side until the flesh is cooked and translucent.

4 Pour a pool of sauce onto each serving plate and place a red snapper fillet on top. Scatter with shredded red chilli and chives, and serve hot with lime wedges.

sesame spicy shrimp with pineapple

SERVES two | 250 | 10 | 2

Prep: **20** mins Chill: **1** hr

250 g/9 oz cooked, peeled large prawns
2 tablespoons lemon juice
2 tablespoons orange juice
1 tablespoon dark rum
½ small pineapple
a little freshly grated nutmeg
coriander leaves, to garnish

Sesame marinade:

2 tablespoons sweet chilli sauce
2 tablespoons rice vinegar or cider vinegar
2 tablespoons orange juice
2 teaspoons soy sauce
1 teaspoon brown sugar
1 teaspoon ginger purée
2 teaspoons toasted sesame seeds

1 Mix together all the sesame marinade ingredients in a bowl and add the cooked prawns. Turn them in the marinade to coat them, then cover and chill in the refrigerator for at least 1 hour.

2 Mix the lemon and orange juice with the rum. Cut a pineapple in half and trim the end and sides to remove the hard outer skin. Cut the flesh into wedges and place in the citrus rum mixture. Cover and chill for at least 30 minutes.

3 Arrange the pineapple wedges around 2 serving plates and sprinkle with nutmeg. Pile the marinated prawns in the centre and scatter with coriander leaves. Serve with a crisp salad.

SERVES two | 400 | 16 | 9

cajun blackened steak with spicy wedges

Prep: **15** mins Cook: **15-20** mins

2 x 150 g/5 oz lean fillet steaks, all visible fat removed
2 medium pink sweet potatoes
spray oil
½ teaspoon ground coriander
½ teaspoon ground cumin
pinch of ground cardamom
sea salt crystals
watercress and sliced oranges, to serve

Cajun seasoning:

½ teaspoon cayenne pepper
1 teaspoon paprika
1 teaspoon allspice
½ teaspoon garlic powder
salt and freshly ground black pepper
½ teaspoon dried oregano

1 Mix together the ingredients for the cajun seasoning and press it into both sides of the fillet steaks. Set aside in the refrigerator or a cool place while you prepare the sweet potatoes.

2 Parboil the whole unpeeled sweet potatoes in their skin in a pan of boiling water for 10 minutes or until just tender. Remove and cool slightly.

3 Cut the cooled sweet potatoes into wedges and spray lightly with oil. Sprinkle with the ground spices and then cook on a hot barbecue or a griddle pan for a few minutes each side until crisp and golden. Sprinkle with a little sea salt.

4 While the potato wedges are cooking, grill the steaks on a hot griddle pan or under a preheated grill until cooked to your liking - 3 minutes each side for rare; 4 minutes each side for medium rare; 6 minutes each side for well done.

5 Serve the steaks and sweet potato wedges with some watercress topped with sliced oranges.